Lowballer

Lowballer

Kim Goodliffe

DEMETER PRESS, BRADFORD, ONTARIO

Canada Council   Conseil des Arts
for the Arts   du Canada

The publisher gratefully acknowledges the support of the Canada Council for the Arts for its publishing program.

Demeter Press
c/o Motherhood Initiative for Research and
 Community Involvement (MIRCI)
140 Holland St. West, P.O. 13022
Bradford, ON, L3Z 2Y5
Telephone: 905.775.9089
Email: info@demeterpress.org
Website: www.demeterpress.org

Demeter Press logo based on the sculpture, "Demeter" by Maria-Luise Bodirsky <www.keramik-atelier.bodirsky.de>

Front cover artwork:
Laurie Papou, "she wished she had been named Hope as a reminder," 2000, oil on wood panel, 67.75 x 48.5 in. From the collection Vanity Suite.

Library and Archives Canada Cataloguing in Publication

Goodliffe, Kim, 1967–
   Lowballer : poems by Kim Goodliffe

ISBN 978-1-927335-23-9

Cataloguing data available from Library and Archives Canada.

Printed and Bound in Canada

MIX
Paper from
responsible sources
FSC® C004071

For Daphne Marlatt,
who suggested that I could *Let language go
where language wants to go.*

Day 1

Sinking into red
plush chairs, I inhale
a forest's spruce air, lick
simulated butter
from my fingers.

Close-up owls
blink, cut
to pounding
moose hooves
a brown meadow,
pan up to lurching
racks of antennae.

The film breaks, you
hold my right hand
the projector's beam
a flurry of dust, sees me
slip in and out of
forest borders
planting trees like
orange marigolds, organized,
a sunny field of corn
once glimpsed from
a freeway

Day 2

We thunder past
stations, hurtle
head over heels
and everyone knows, we're
groping each other under
my sleeping bag.

Soon we will live
together, chokecherry
blossoms and Pink Lady's Slipper
slip in and out
of our cozy tent
the borders of Eden
will open, soon you say
you will pick me berries.

How sweet, the train blasts
its horn, we French kiss, unzip
each other's pants, on our
escape to Northern blossoms.

Day 3

Check list:
raincoat, rain pants
thermal underwear
ten pairs socks, sweaters
t-shirts, turtlenecks
Balaclava, sun hat
swimsuit, rubber
gloves, steel-shafted safety
boots, duct tape, tent
tarp, Thermarest
rope, sleeping
bag, plate
bowl, cup
cutlery, flashlight
Band-Aids, batteries
sunscreen, Muskol
calamine lotion,
Walkman, Swiss Army
knife, toiletries, tapes:
The Breeders, Pond
Cocteau Twins
birth control,
Bear Spray.

Day 4

We are packed into the van –
gear, one woman and six men
pass a haze of orange
reeking pulp and bleach.

One peeled strip of
highway divides
creeping bush, bare granite
juts into hills, expands in a
torn shag of trees, look
a hawk! and another
five in just ten minutes.

We veer left, witness
the first logging road's crush –
trees shaved brown, jagged
machinery rips off limbs
bunches, peels and
stacks the blue horizon flat.

Land at camp –
a gravel pit, dotted with
sci-fi silver trailers, half-bubble
neon tents.

I disembark, test the air
take the first step for man-
kind, Moosewood
Reforestation.

Day 5

You know a music
that stops the loon's swallowed cackle
in the back of my mouth,
tickles my throat into laughing,
into frequencies that mosquitoes,
circles in water, the tree
itching in my hand
thrill to run through.

Day 6

After another day of lowballing
I retreat into (y)our tent
sharing half-zippered sleep
trapped breathing
dew on the dome ceiling

what forms on the inside of your eyes
is what forms on the inside of my eyes –
reflex dream of boot and shovel
blurring in a landscar.

Slipping through each other's borders
no lock, no key,
nobody fits entirely in
without spilling out
into the next planter
                    the next tent
                              the next furrow
                                        the next block.

By morning you uncurl –
lean in and pull back
on a fulcrum of ego
the way a steel-toed boot supports
a shovel.

When I emerge
from behind our flap of vinyl,
who comes out
might be any collection of us here,
hail, sunshine or rain.

Day 7

Morning's first primal scream,
cook's alarm-clock spoon
banging a garbage can lid,
unlaced boots
stumble by.

On top of our wet sleeping bag
you shiver
inside three layers
of clothing.

You don't know you make the sound
of a small animal, or why you are pulled
to the magnet outside.

Arthritic shovel hand
unzips metal teeth
highballer body
squeezes out tent door.

My voice whispers
Stay down.

The fly on the tent
flaps slow motion signals,
rain drums on tight vinyl
pulling veins across the roof.

I survey parts.

What used to be knees,
hands, are flares
pulsing

don't
don't you dare
move.

Day 8

11 trays.

770 trees @ .07
$58.80
camp costs
-$22.00

My total
$31.90.

35 trays.

2450 trees @ .07
$171.50
camp costs
-$22.00

Your total
$149.50.

Day 9

In a private moment
pants at my ankles, insects'
delight.

A dozen wooden sponge-tongues
drenched in ivy, curl
stretch to catch
a few drops of urine.

Spring taste of wind, birds
plunge down
touch each nipple shape of
truth, furred green breasts
half-sunk in a bed of sphagnum.

Enthralled by a trunk's downward thrust
suggestions spread themselves green
open, quietly enmeshed
in a system of roots' twirled bones
fluid seeking everywhere –

fingers on fingers and hairs.

Day 10

MUSKOL
INSECT REPELLENT

CAUTION POISON
read label before using
50 ml skull and crossbones
provides up to 8 hours protection
from mosquitoes and black flies.

Wash or wipe palms after applying.

KEEP OUT
OF REACH OF CHILDREN.
DO NOT USE
ON INFANTS AND TODDLERS.
Do not take internally.

RARE [it says] SIDE EFFECTS
clumsiness, confusion,
convulsions, loss
of consciousness
slurred speech, unusual
tiredness or weakness.

Day 11

In the swamp
when the swarm comes
I resist

wrap clothing on my head
the swirling mass trapped inside
like a living turban, I resist
a thick wall of buzzing, biting.

I scream
slap my face
hurt myself
the first time
I cry.

Then quiet
submission
absorbed by them
the idea of hunger, the
idea of sacrifice.

Day 12

A warning rifle fires
in early evening light, I throw down
my mystery novel, press nose into fine mesh window –
a bear on hind legs
claws open flimsy metal,
upturned mouth gulps Coleman fuel,
throws the hollow can down, drops onto all fours,
sniffs up and down
searching for what?
I can't breathe
or turn away.

Its heavy head angles left, draws an ambling body
to the cook trailer window –
punches in, pulls out a potato
a rifle blasts,
bear springs into four-legged gallop –
a free/carbo-loader.

Days Off

Slugs

i
Androgynous baby of the dried plum
the slow snail who left everything behind
peeled away lychee layer,
a simple dark stone
melted in moonlight.

ii
With the laser eyes of science,
you broke a finger
off the arm of a cedar
and poked into black silk.

We watched the body pour away
slow as honey,
fluid as instinct.

iii
Every slug has a story
remember Peter's wife who wept
inside the pumpkin
squeezed through rot black walls
a shrunken body
to shimmy in the open breeze.

She undulates, pauses
moves on.

To stop is to harden
settle for mushroom loneliness.

iv
The fears
nameless, immense and soft.
Deep puddles, prodding
tongues of moose, deer
a slow moist crush.

The pleasures
a light drizzle
antenna reaching
a mirrored muscle
inside gelatin skin.

v
Progress
the constant inching
over a forest path
mouthbody puckered, sucking
for mother, brother
sister, father
anything that feels like inside
but is not.

vi
I tell you
Not everything has a voice.

*

WRESTLE CESAR THE BEAR
ONE NIGHT ONLY, DON'T MISS
CANADA'S BIGGEST BLACK BEAR
800 pounds, the Star Strip Club
Saturday, 8PM, TEN BUCKS A
WRESTLE, FIVE BUCKS AT THE DOOR
beer lover's special
Ex on tap.

(Wet t-shirt contest canceled)

*

Paws bandaged in hockey tape,
plastic muzzle strapped
tight to the sloped head.

CESAR slumps
an indifferent fur boulder
eyes glazed, staring
at slats of sun
through bent Venetian blinds,
caught
on mirrored walls
blind (I hope)
if we look too long.

But no, you're the first on stage
hands in hockey gloves
ears and eyes caged in a goalie mask
twenty beer drinkers
cheer, you ram,
try to flip the massive bear
on its back.

Please, I'll have a third,
low-cut waitress
pulls a frosty beer
from the dripping tray
the bills she returns
are wet and soft,
the sun fades
on the mirrored wall.

CESAR stands
hugs you tight
flips you down
the first contestant
(s)he's sat on tonight.

What a match, folks
what a match.

Day 13

Inside the rattling of metal
we crawl

6:30 AM
music blares, rocks strike
the van's thin shell

through the gap in the back doors
dust filters in, don't think
last season
veered into a ditch –
shovel chopped skull
one died: the rules changed
secure all shovels
firmly on the outside.

To my right the valley trembles
behind glass, scarified rows
a hundred dirt rivers
flow into snarled mountains
a million tangled possibilities:
twisted ankle? broken leg
falling forward on a sharp stick?
one eye pierced,
the forever wink
that would get me out of here.

Day 14

Green Jello, oh
again, a silver spoon
the go whistle, you shove'n'shovel
sweet flesh, the flavour of green
muscle, the soft emerald
shine on a chipped plate.

Win a 26 oz. bottle of
rum-yo-ho-ho and a –
ten, eleven seconds, twelve
Jello eating contests, again
the trailer door glints open
green iridescent swallows
flying sweet, fourteen
fifteen hustlers
count aloud for a bottle of rum.

Day 15

I reach for a shovel
my hand snaps off
I reach for your hand but
twigs, a rib bone, a broken shovel
(or I reach for your hand but find
my own, snapped off
when I met you)

In the dream the light
shuts off.

If we're not planting
we must be hiding.

Day 16

On the hottest day yet
instead of instructions,
sighs and grunts
you waited,
gave me
one small organ laid flat in your hand.

Hot juice eased the ache in my throat
pulled me down to my knees
reaching for
more of what I didn't know I wanted

now exposed,
obvious in dusty green leaves,
wild strawberries.

One by one
the crew was drawn to us,
crouched down in three furrows
seven men/one woman
stillness beating on our tongues
while the landscape filled the movie screen
over, under, around us.

This was the only work
break we could all agree on.

Day 17

Gun
fire as
we read
in (y)our little
orange tent with
claw cuts resewn
in diagonal swipes
along front and back
walls where the bear got
in last year on days off, Cook

screaming outside, MNR brought the
damn live trap, wouldn't let me sign for it,
tried gettin'em to stay for dinner so a boss
could sign but they refused, loaded up that trap,
gotta take the three-hour trip right then, the way
they just came, those Suits scared of drivin' in the dark
bears don't got a chance, damnation & ruination, a curse
to the logging camp with the open dump, those mean fucks...

by morning the big boss had already shot two in camp & nobody
would move them in the heat the bitter smells of death the circling
vultures bend to in the heat I tried to get pot to stop the rising despair I
couldn't feel so uncomfortable for another night but
no pot, the
acid also
eaten.

Day 18

Is it only me who can't stop listening?

This same hot wind that
blows in my ears
bends the spines of the mojos
moaning like witches over my furrow
a chicken hawk hisses
beside her nest
I don't know how long
I've been away

I search out patterns –
rivers and cracks filled with dirt
my hands, each stained lifeline aging
what I used to be

I sniff hot spruce citrus and earth,
magic spell that unsnaps my planting bags
lays me down to rest in you, old friend.

Day 19

11 trays.

770 trees @ .07
$58.80
camp costs
-$22.00

My total
$31.90.

38 trays.

2660 trees @ .07
$186.20
camp costs
-$22.00

Your total
$164.20.

Days Off

Garter Snake

i

Escaped sister of the garden hose
slithering over the gravel drive
the tough skinned soul
pulling tight against
self-loathing
perfect recoil
from Eden.

Ears scraped clean, through
centuries of neglect she
listens to no one but
her own instincts a quick
fuck in late fall a frog –
prince she stuns, balances
need in her jaws
and swallows.

ii

The nightmares are cold –
flung against rock, the shovel
chop or trapped
flying in a hawk's
beak, she tells
no one, would rather
join Medusa
than know pity

iii
Pleasure's self-taught
rill

accepted gravity's pull
since the first curled ride
out of mother's egg.

A lone synergy, a
hundred ribbed muscles
swimming land, sand
mud.

Mouth opens to
smell earth
worm, to
taste.

iv
Sun grips the
length of her body –

brief discomfort as
skin sloughs
over hard
disc eyes

then swift movement
like wind in the tall grass.

Day 20

CAUTION
unusual tiredness or weakness

REPELLENT
8 hours protection

RARE internal SIDE EFFECTS
confusion, slurred speech, projection
nausea, romantic fantasies, internal bleeding

APPLY SPARINGLY
(copiously)

Day 21

Approaching the tree cache, it's hard to believe
a cub pulls your purple backpack from the van window.

It's hard to believe your order,
We gotta get that pack,
back.

Hard, climbing over slash,
making noise, clapping confusion
screaming intimidation in pursuit of
the bear perched on a log, eating an orange.

We are gaining,
you throw a shovel
the cub, a black blur flies up a slash pile.

You rifle through your backpack,
desperate for insulin,
tear into an orange.

Light headed, *Sugar,* you declare,
I'm gonna get that bear.

Day 22

I O U $80 (broke
your Ray-Bans)

18 trays

1260 trees

$88.20
$88.20
$88.20.

Day 23

One kick
with a work boot

the furry body
jiggles,

ears still perky
pink tongue lolling
between gummy black lips.

I hold a paw
run fingers over
rough pads.

Bend down to sniff where
she has traveled.

You walk away
rifle slung over shoulder.

Day 24

You've broken the mirror, I
see myself in puddles
mudhead joined with clouds
pockmarked with rain, my
opinion of myself is
my opinion of dark clouds, nothing
but a hot or cold body to
react to, evaporate on.

Day 25

The sky ripped open
inside of us
insects, dirt followed.

It's getting worse –
at night, dreams
twist spruce arrows
out of my hands
your mouth
the hard, cracked jaws of clay
trails torn, grub roots.

Is that your face or mine
spilling from its edges
from what used to be
the whites of eyes, teeth
every feature warps unfamiliar
doubled in the heat
and glaring sun.

I can't wait for you to rescue me I
can't wait for you to rescue me any more.

We're crouched in a deep furrow
the earth rises missile slow
folding over our shoulders
a blanket that brings no comfort
but at least something other
than work, prayer.

Day 26

Despite callouses, pesticide
rash, you're still graced
with that delicate
touch.

So gentle
you hold the deer-
fly's buzzing body,

shove a
pine needle up its
ass! quick
release and giggle
at the corkscrew flight.

Day 27

Like my shovel
I am blunt
around the edges

the more force I use,
the duller I become

every day I
hit rock bottom

pain explodes my arms
catch fire with mosquitoes.

The morning line up
to sharpen shovels
grows longer, quieter.

Blue-white sparks break and shatter,
squeal with the concentration
of wearing metal down
to a fine point
of entry.

Days Off

*

It's the day shift, the night shift
of living with men
of eating the pork and Jello of them.

It's the name the boss gives us
like Mac, Moose or Beaver
still fingering me in the phosphate river.

It's the line up, cat calls
the countdown, heatstroke
the weak-kneed, less than
scaredy-cat cunt.

It's the bonespurs, bleachwater
catcall, the lowball –
and I blame myself
not the weather.

Not the duff kick
or bear trap.

It's self-bait
takes me screaming
through their big bush.

*

We range westward from
New Brunswick to BC, migrate
April to September
south of the tree-line,
bush to town, motel
to motel to motel.

Identifiable markings –
zinc-striped cheeks, tye-dyed
bandana, patches of milk-silver
duct tape, all varieties
of skin under the sun.

Small towns witness our
dramatic mid-summer descent –
groups of 4 to 10
orange vans hump
logging roads, highways
pour into liquor store
parking lots, where we alight
parched and prepared
to drink
48 to 72 hours.

The male's distinctive cry –
a two-syllabic yee-haw
repeats anywhere
from 4 to 27 times.

Otherwise the sexes are indistinguishable.
Favour dance floors
stolen heavy machinery
(when accessible) motel rooms'
puke-encrusted bed sheets.

Near-conscious mating may occur
accidentally at any time
in this thirsty season.

Signs of our departure
unmistakable –
clusters of crushed beer tins, soggy
chip bags, Trojan Shields
motel office signs'
punched through words, *No*
Tree Planters.

Day 29

What used to hold me together was
skin, bone, muscle

now sharp sticks
puncture illusions,
liver, spleen,
uterus and heart.

Blisters on my finger tips
fill like ticks,
pop and tear.

Now androgynous in Sally Ann clothing
strips of duct tape fly from my shirt.

In this block I become
clear cut,
leveled of questions,
barreling over what remains
my only purpose at this moment
to plant

(7 cents)
3 steps forward
open earth
plant Jack pine
7 plus 7
3 steps forward
open earth
plant Jack pine
7 plus 7 plus
plus plus.

Day 31

Together, we enter
lock the shower stall door

warm water
pours from a black bag

you're not all mean
you scrub my back

a cube of ivory
melts in your hands

our eyes close,
heads rise with a simple wish –

insects, blood, pesticide, lotion
slide,
pool at our feet.

In my hand, a drop of green
Clairol Herbal Essence

foams your long black hair
eyes phosphoresce

my deep sea creature
my frog prince, kiss

this bubble
rising from my mouth.

Day 33

Ramming shovel in –
goddamn hard clay

(on a hot day, red skin
sent out flares in the afternoon).

Done all kinds of –
done bush work, damnit –
brushing, jesus, this is –
fuck this.

Walking away down a logging road
your head shaking words
to a groaning song

I pretend not to recognize
though we all know the tune

caught in every throat
the tune that wants
to protect self
from breaking self.

Your shovel flew
just beyond the tree cache,
where your hard-hat also crashed.

From a short distance,
self-destructing
from the outside in
sounds like
bullshit –
collapsed in a ditch
sobbing by the
logging road at
10:30 AM.

Day 34

You didn't throw the shovel *at*
but *towards* me
a distinction that keeps me
schizoid in time and place.

A tremble in my gut,
the wind rolls a broken shrub
across the road
where sedimentary layers ripple
inside hardened granite,

Words petrify,
close in on themselves
in the few seconds before
I'm about to feel,
a warning from the past
presses against my rib cage,
the need to be quiet
and careful.

You walk towards me –
the shovel,
in the few seconds
before I'm about to
feel, my fingers tear away,
weightless in time
and space, escaping into
the one second
before I'm about to feel,
they light
a Malboro Light.

I inhale,
smoke ripples
from my mouth.

Day 36

All day in the planting block,
train schedules rattle
in dirt, rock, my head:

      could hitch a ride on a
                     logging truck
      get a lift with the
                     new camp cook
      she leaves on Wednesday for the
                     liquor store
      in town, walk straight to the
                     bus depot
      sit on a beautiful
                     wooden bench,
      in a florescent
                     light buzz.

Instead we go on planting
ride back to base camp
behind bug-smeared glass
ignoring blocks of Martian suburbs.

Day 39

22 trays.
540 trees.
$107.80.

Minus $190.00 for my
shovel, my bags.

Minus $95.00 for the
train ticket home.

Minus $12 000.00 for (Oh)
my Canada and
provincial student loan.

Minus. Mine us. Mine.

Day 40

The boulder drops a piece of itself
to the earth, I gasp

the thud, vibrating
up booted feet, tissues, bones in
legs and hips, the sheared basin rock
rocking organs, belly, up lungs and ribs
my heart, flutters, startled
nervous system
sparked and floodshocked.

A boulder's hairline fracture
and I take a centuries-long exhale.

This grey flecked rock fluid,
it is me who is petrified.

Day 41

Our construction hats clink –
plastic, yellow as Fisher Price toys.

We sit side by side
jangled with the van's descent
into potholes, some questions
I don't ask, stare at
imitation green
leather upholstery
on the seat in front
cracked and intricate
as my calloused hands.

Tentatively, you steer your head left with
the word *sorry*
wait for me to
forgive you, the term you've
repeated over years, until its meaning is
lost. Today
I refuse.

Gas fumes invade
the air I breathe in
hold as long as I
can, birds
unheard in the machine noise
start from the bushes
fly off.

Days Off

*

Waking up, a dandelion
hangs over me,
head tilted, searching
its hot likeness.

Moist yellow
spear-tipped petals
my fingers find
fine hairs, the stem
firmly planted in grass.

The lawnmower roars,
I sit up, my head
split in two,
a man next door
shaves green
electric strips,
the green smell
churns stomach acid
my splitting head
barely attached
on someone's front lawn.

Day 50

Zero fire tolerance –
24 degrees, *no smokes in the block
or poof,* the crew boss says
break now
under the silver safety
tarp strapped to the van.
If the heat rises
one more degree, a button, a
glint of windshield will
catch this tinder forest.

Quiet we breathe
the crickets' drugged mantra
through still crackle and dust
swallow only hot pink-
flavoured Kool-Aid, sweat
clean. The silver tarp
flaps once, immense
pleasure thrills every
body hair, we have never
rested together
without words, quotas we
cling to cool dirt, finally
conquered, stifled.

Day 53

In the tent's slow heat we
sprawl on two islands of vinyl,
twin survivors.

A breeze
evaporates sweat.

You sigh –
pine-green thunder
cracks the canopy of the
sky, your skin
flickers in burst lightning.

A shadow of us
ripples down the dome –
my head, my body spills
on your body,
hands, arms dissolve
each breast in your mouth
pulsing rain drops, we
gasp in this half bubble,
ride each wave and crash.

Day 55

You and I tangle
like the furrows of this ripped up land –
to make sense is to pretend
there is a plan.

We chew gum to
the rhythm of new anxieties –
a distant rifle fires,
quiets a blue-black raven
mid-hop in the railway tracks.

Our mouths sucked dry
with dust, everything
flies invisible.

We keep them firmly shut
until the ride home.

To drink water is to lose
money/sanity.

"You must understand
this is seasonal work."

Day 56

You breathed out
through what was impenetrable,
drew a cloud of black no-see-ums
against the mosquito net.

Who could calculate that small galaxy
with it's microscopic spaces,
filaments swarmed to your magnet mouth,
the night not yet dark,
the book I pretended to read all summer
closed.

My ears unhinged
in the cellophane drizzle
of insect bodies
ticking against
the invisible walls
where we lived,

each small acknowledgment
hurling desire,
& yet separate
from the source
you pronounced
Carbon Dioxide
to no one in particular.

Day 57

One hour ago, in a furrow on a hill
I stopped
cried rain from the frames of my eyes.

Feelings, I don't deserve,
the work is punishment
enough –

Back on my feet,
storm through slash,
work slams shovel into clay
tree-hand plucks tree
from left hip bag
tree after tree
I half-bury in earth
until empty beyond language
finally equal to/no better than
three gangly bear cubs
clinging to three thin trees,
a cloud rips, electric buzz
of a red-winged blackbird
wild intelligence of the body.

In hard land
I bag two thousand eight hundred,
return to camp
where everyone asks
how much
blood/money
highballers applaud, hit me
that afternoon
on the back,
pronounce me
highest high-
baller of the day.

Day 58

Instead of rubbing my shoulders
you tally numbers,
unzip our shared lair,
create your own pod.

I'm tired of waiting for a
kind word, a sip of
cool water, some
sign of life other than a look that says,
one wrong move, I will
devour you.

Not blood and flesh,
RARE [it says] SIDE EFFECTS
clumsiness, confusion,
convulsions, loss
of consciousness
slurred speech, unusual
tiredness or weakness.

I sniff the air
where you disappeared.

My fingernails have peeled away
leaving tender baby stubs
what will I fight you with
now that I have to?

Day 60

Forty-two trays too much
after ten straight days hard labour

body weaker than
the rational anthem: nothing worse than being here than
being here not making money,

enough, I take the shrink-wrapped cube
packed tight with
1008 baby black spruce,
        weight the burden down
    with rocks
drag it into Go Home Lake,
I sink and
drown the load

(the struggle
between
man [sic]
and nature).

This stash,
Illegal, secret
allows a few hours, paid
to lay in the cool sighing moss.

Day 61

Breathless
on the shore
with crew #4

metres from my
thousand dollar fine
stash of baby spruce
shrink-wrapped and lying on the bottom.

Hoping plastic lasts forever, and gravity
works in my favour
as the crew jumps

screaming
kicking & pissing
in Go Home Lake.

I stand and scan the surface.

What I tried to bury,
now freed of soil plugs
floats to the surface,
a sudden infestation.

Days Off

*

Except for the welts
on my ears and neck,
the ringing of metal
hitting rock inside,
nothing betrays my former line of
work, crime, dismissal.

The clean train hums
straight clean walls, I vibrate
on a cushioned seat, hand
the man my ticket to ride.

But inside
where the sky used to wag kites, birds
I feel the boiled eyeball of the sun
not rising or setting
but enough of a threat to split open
my history.

*

Before we turned against each other
shut down programming for the day
and ended with a rainbow high-
pitched test pattern
before we bled each other dry
before we made each other
incommunicable monsters
before you failed to be my superhero

before we turned to beer, pot, rock
cryptonite, first at the head
slowly creeping down
into the flesh of our four feet
splintering in gravity, before
we stopped scraping our bodies
against each other, feeding time
and space the desire of our minds
to be right, before you broke
your word, implosion, before
the wind storm ripped
our tent from the earth, and we
shivered, wrapped in blankets
orphans again.

*

Pieces I've lost
replaced with –

tangled slash, deer
flash of silver
water cloud of
parasites naked
humans howl in a
cold green river
clean hieroglyphics
of pink flagging tape
defines blocks
memory's improved
continuum where
you toil still
7 cents, hitting rock
blood, sweat and

            foreign.

Territory, my mind
I've done time in
swallowed every lie,
various insects, pioneers
glossed over.

*

A cafe newspaper
wilts in my hands
single white male
enjoys romantic strolls?
perfectly bitter
cup of coffee
half drunk, cooling
nearing the end of the
want ads, I peel apart
pages, bodies evade
the window, blinding
in the sun glare, please
show up so I can leave
you, coffee
breathes through me, soft
toxic moss on my tongue
percolates through skin, sweating
naked on the beach
first kiss, *there is nothing
we can't work out*, hiss of
espresso steam cloud
disappears, another ten minutes

the empty chair, I can't
argue with, wooden,
perfectly balanced, my
smudged fingerprints cling
to the borders of
stories, my horoscope
says I'm a born
leader, waiting,
at the cafe.

Acknowledgements

Note for Found Poem "Muskol": Information was found on a Muskol label and on the web site for the makers of Muskol: Schering-Plough Healthcare.

Earlier versions of these poems appeared in *Descant, Filling Station and Milieu Press*. My thanks to the editors of each.

Thanks to the participants, faculty and staff of the Banff Centre for the Arts 2001, and especially to Daphne Marlatt.

To Angela Royea, for her intelligent editing and support.

To the Rubus Collective – Leslie Palleson, Dilara Ally and Lissa Cowan – for ongoing inspiration and creative entanglement.

To Andrea O'Reilly at Demeter Press, for her vision to explore Mothering in all its forms.

To Yvonne Blomer of the Planet Earth Poetry series for maintaining a vital poetry scene in Victoria.

To the 5 Rhythms tribe, and especially to Lisa Weeks.

And to my mom, for dreaming aloud in December.

Originally from Scarborough, Kim Goodliffe planted trees in the Lake-of-the-Woods region during a bear "infestation." Her poetry, short fiction and non-fiction have appeared in Canadian literary magazines and newspapers including *Descant, Grain, subTerrain, Vancouver Review* and the *Vancouver Sun*. She holds an MFA in creative writing from the University of British Columbia.